This book
belongs to:

....

....

LET'S TALK

My friend has Down's syndrome

Written by Jennifer Moore-Mallinos

Illustrated by Marta Fàbrega

BOOK HOUSE

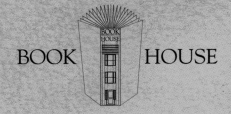

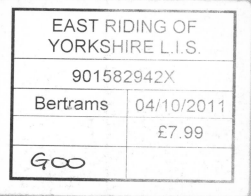

Do you have a special friend?

I do! Her name is Ella, and she's my best friend. I met Ella last summer at the Fun Club that runs through the school holidays. I've been going to the club every year, but last summer was the best ever because that's when I met Ella.

Last summer's Fun Club started out just like it did every year. All the kids were divided into three groups. There was a group of little kids, a group of big kids and a group in the middle. I was in the middle group of kids who were seven, eight, or nine years old, because I was eight.

Each group had a club leader. My club leader was Miss Theresa. She was really nice! Every day she found fun things for us to do, like treasure hunts or swimming. Sometimes we played volleyball on the beach or tag, and every Friday we did arts and crafts. Also, last summer was the first year that we all got to be in a talent show, even the little kids!

At the end of the first week at the club Miss Theresa told us that there was going to be someone new joining our group and that her name was Ella. Miss Theresa said that she was going to need our help to make Ella feel welcome and that she wanted one of us to be Ella's special buddy while she learned the ropes.

When Miss Theresa asked me if I wanted to be Ella's buddy I was so excited! I'd been to the club more often than the rest of the group, so she thought that I was the best person for the job.

Miss Theresa said that even though Ella would spend most of her time with me, she expected the whole group to be patient and understanding because Ella had Down's syndrome. She said that it meant that Ella might need extra help with some of the activities we did, especially the talent show.

We were all a bit scared because we didn't know much about Down's syndrome. One of the boys was worried that we might all catch it from Ella and that maybe it wasn't a good idea to have her in our group. Someone else wondered if Ella should go to a special club instead of ours, especially since she might need extra help.

Miss Theresa said that the Fun Club was for all kids and that included children like Ella.

She told us that children born with Down's syndrome have something extra in their bodies. Inside our bodies are trillions of cells, and inside each cell are even smaller things called chromosomes. These are instructions that tell your body how to work. Most people have 46 sets of instructions but Ella has 47.

Miss Theresa said that children with Down's syndrome have special features. Their faces are a bit larger and flatter than ours and they have almond-shaped eyes, and smaller mouths and ears. Their arms and legs are usually a bit shorter, too. Some children with Down's syndrome may have trouble hearing or seeing things well, and some may take longer to learn to do some things. But the difficulties that children with Down's syndrome sometimes have do not stop them from having the same hopes and dreams as us.

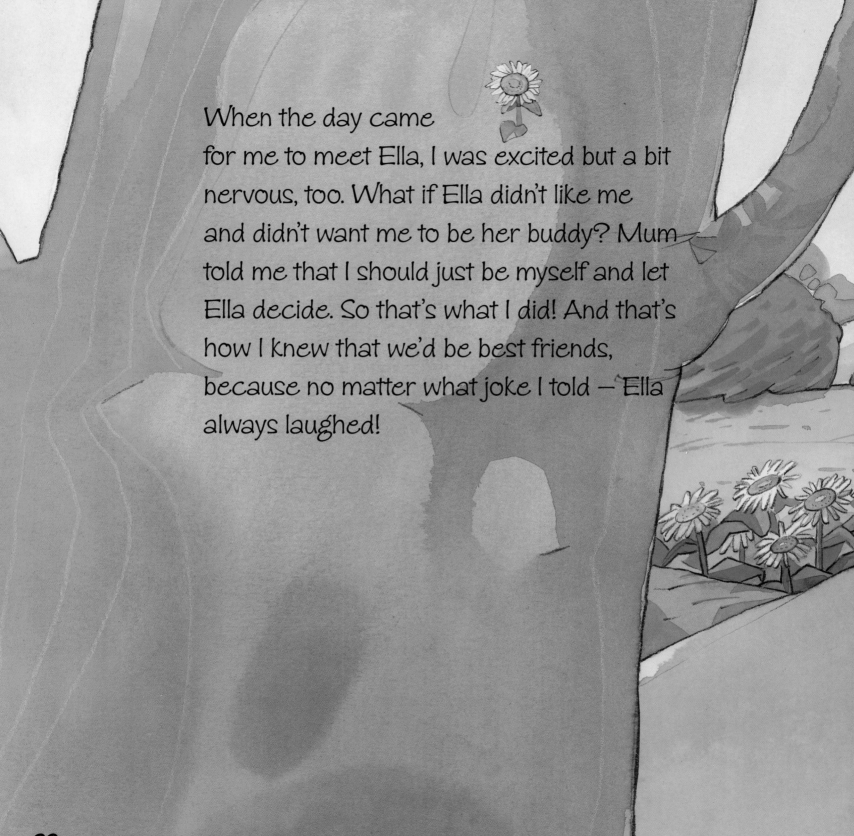

When the day came
for me to meet Ella, I was excited but a bit
nervous, too. What if Ella didn't like me
and didn't want me to be her buddy? Mum
told me that I should just be myself and let
Ella decide. So that's what I did! And that's
how I knew that we'd be best friends,
because no matter what joke I told — Ella
always laughed!

Ella was a bit slower at some of the sports that we did, like running races and tag, but she was good at other things. She was really good at arts and crafts, especially pottery. Ella could mould a blob of clay into anything, even pretty plates and vases! And when it was time for the talent show I felt so shy that I wanted to quit, but Ella helped me to be brave and didn't let me give up.

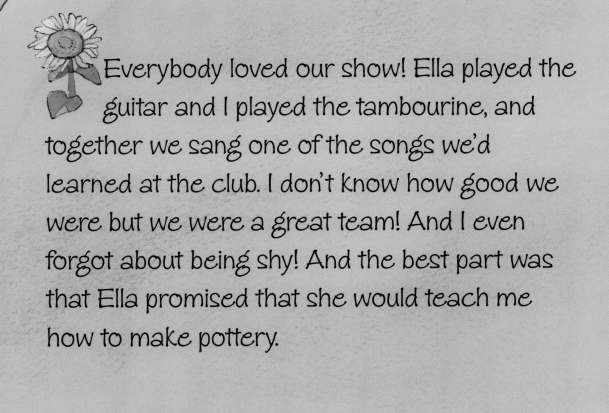

Everybody loved our show! Ella played the guitar and I played the tambourine, and together we sang one of the songs we'd learned at the club. I don't know how good we were but we were a great team! And I even forgot about being shy! And the best part was that Ella promised that she would teach me how to make pottery.

Ella and I have been friends ever since that first day we met at the club and just as she promised, she's teaching me how to make pottery now. Just like Ella, I need help with a lot of things too! And that's OK!

29

Note to Parents

The purpose of this book is to acknowledge the existence of Down's syndrome among children and to eliminate existing barriers between these children and their peers. It also attempts to make readers aware that children diagnosed with Down's syndrome have the potential and ability to become active participants among their peers and within society.

It is hoped that this book will promote a better understanding and acceptance of all children!

According to the Down's syndrome Association, about two Down's syndrome babies are born each day and there are currently about 60,000 people in the UK who have Down's syndrome.

Down's syndrome is a genetic condition in which a person is born with an extra 21st chromosome, giving a total of 47 chromosomes rather than 46. Although Down's syndrome cannot be prevented, it can be detected during pregnancy.

Down's syndrome was first comprehensively described and identified by Dr John Langdon Down in a paper that he published in 1866; however, it was not until 1959 that the extra chromosome was detected.

Children with Down's syndrome share certain facial and physical features such as a flat facial profile, an upward slant to the eyes, an enlarged tongue and a single crease across the centre of their palms. Although many children with Down's syndrome grow at a slower rate, they are able to reach developmental milestones. Many children with Down's syndrome are shorter than their peers of similar age.

Cognitive development often varies among individuals; however, most have mild to moderate impairments. These children may have delays in speech, fine and gross motor skills, and may mature at a slower pace in regard to their emotional, social and intellectual development.

Some children may experience congenital heart defects, as well as hearing and visual impairment. These audio and visual deficits often affect a child's language and learning skills.

More frequent health conditions that occur in children with Down's syndrome include thyroid problems, intestinal abnormalities, respiratory problems, obesity, an increased vulnerability to infections, and a higher risk of childhood leukemia. Some children may also experience seizures.

However, some people with Down's syndrome may not have any of these health problems.

Individuals with Down's syndrome have become accepted members of our society. Many opportunities are available for them to lead full and rewarding lives. Recreational, educational and social programmes give individuals the chance to develop their skills and abilities, while providing them with the opportunity to discover hidden talents. Many children with Down's syndrome now go to their local mainstream school. However, some children will find that a special school is better for them. It all depends on the needs of the individual child.

Parents who learn that their child has Down's syndrome will often experience a range of emotions. Finding the appropriate information and support networks available within your community helps to alleviate many of these initial concerns.

There are many intervention programmes available for your child, and some of these should match your child's individual needs. Some children may require physical, speech and occupational assistance as well as specialised educational programs.

Many children with Down's syndrome are active members of our society. Many will go on to complete further education courses after leaving school. Young people with Down's syndrome are able to find employment and live independently.

All children deserve a chance to get the most out of life and to develop lasting relationships. Perhaps, by breaking down some of the barriers that exist between all children, every child, no matter what, will strive for excellence and become the best that he or she can be!

Consultant:
Stuart Mills has worked for the
Down's Syndrome Association as
an Information Officer for 11 years.

www.downs-syndrome.org.uk

Other titles in this series:

Lost and found

Have you got a secret?

I remember

Published in Great Britain in MMXII by
Book House, an imprint of
The Salariya Book Company Ltd
25 Marlborough Place, Brighton BN1 1UB
www.salariya.com
www.book-house.co.uk

1 3 5 7 9 8 6 4 2

A CIP catalogue record for this book is available
from the British Library.

Printed and bound in China.

PB ISBN: 978-1-908177-08-7

Original title of the book in Spanish: Mi amiga tiene el síndrome de Down
© Copyright MMVI by Gemser Publications, S.L.
El Castell, 38; Teià (08329) Barcelona, Spain (World Rights)